Airport Socks

Pages from a
Daughter's Life

Marigene Kowalski

You may contact the author via email at
marigenekowalski@yahoo.com

ISBN: 978-1-66784-145-8 (Print Edition)
ISBN: 978-1-66784-146-5 (eBook Edition)

Dedication

To my good friend, Mary,
who always felt I had a book in me.

Acknowledgment

I wrote this book for my grandson Nicholas,
told through the eyes of his mom,
my daughter, Vicki.

Special Thanks

Thanks to Jefferson for getting
this project off the ground.

Introduction

There is an episode of a very popular 1960s sci-fi TV series in which a salesman walks into a diner carrying a bag containing various articles. He proceeds to hand out the articles to the diners, seemingly at random. During the course of the episode, each diner realizes that they were given exactly what they need to assist them with events that they would experience on that day. This is the premise for the stories that make up *Airport Socks*—pages featuring something about life that I learned at one time or another from my mother, Marigene, and other people.

Once, during my college years, I was preparing for a trip out of the country, and I realized that I lacked a decent carry-on bag. I had always loved the beautiful black one that my mother had splurged on for herself, so I tried my luck. "Mom, if I promise to take care of it, could you spare your travel bag for a week?" Her eyes widened for a couple of seconds, as if she had been stabbed but, in the end, I lucked out. I just had to submit to, "Make sure you don't take it to the beach! The sun will bleach the heck out of it!" While packing it full of the necessary stuff that one includes on a long plane flight, I noticed a pair of short white sport socks at the bottom of the bag. *Hmm*, I thought, *if she gets cold on a plane, wouldn't she just ask for one of those little blankets that they offer you?*

Before I knew it, travel day arrived and there I was in line at the dreaded security check at the airport in New Jersey— wearing my ever-present flip-flops. It was then that I went into full panic: I was going to need to remove them and put my bare feet on the disgusting airport floor! And just then I remembered what was in my mother's carry on. *Airport socks!* As I quickly dug them out, I appreciated that God made mothers. How is it that, most times, they know what you are going to need even before you do?

Family & Friends

My paternal grandparents' wedding, 1947.

Mismatched Dishes

My paternal grandparents were neighbors in their hometown of Bayonne, New Jersey. Back in the day, a guy courted a young lady in person. You went on a walk to get a soda, or sat together sharing thoughts and learning about each other. There were no instant messages or texts—those were pre-cell phone times. In fact, not many homes even had a land line. You had to go down to the corner market to get a message out, and it was usually for something very important. Someone had a baby, someone had a problem … shows you how we take our current instant communication for granted.

Grandma's family lived on the second floor of a two-family house. There were four rooms and a tiny bathroom—no shower stall or tub. In all, there were her parents and seven children. The kids were sent downstairs to their Aunt Mary and Uncle Charlie's place each time the doctor arrived with his black bag to assist in a sibling birth. Grandma used to tell us that she always thought that the new baby had been brought in by the doctor in his bag.

Grandma Victoria and Grandpa Alphonse met when she was helping to translate letters that had come from Poland, addressed to his aunt. It was 1946. Grandpa Al had returned from the Pacific after serving for four years in World War II. Interestingly he was at Pearl Harbor when the Japanese attacked. However, he was in the base hospital recuperating from surgery, and thought that all the commotion in the hallways and outside was merely a military drill.

My grandparents' relationship grew very quickly into love, and they were married on May 25, 1947. The party was held right in the dining room of Grandma's house. Around the table stood the beaming bride and groom, surrounded by members of their family, including Grandpa's brother, Fr. Gene, who had married them. It was a room bursting with happiness and pride. The first time I saw the photograph of the reception, I noticed something that impressed me very much. It was, as they say, my take away, and it was a sign of simpler times. The table was filled to overflowing with multiple plates full of home-made, delicious-looking food. Whenever you produce something homemade, it's done with love behind it and, that day in particular, it showed. Everything was laid out in mismatched but beautiful dishes, proving that you don't need to break the bank to celebrate an event, no matter how important.

The Letter

My father had an aunt who lived with her mother (dad's grandmother) in Bayonne, New Jersey. Aunt Joanna had worked for a manufacturing company in that city. In the 1940s, she met a young man, Walter, at a party. They became fast friends and, before long, the relationship deepened. In 1950 they were married. To quote Aunt Joanna, "I will never forget our wedding day! It was the day of that great hurricane—one of the greatest storms to ever hit Bayonne. There were no lights, and we were married by candlelight. It was thrilling and dramatic." A news website described it as the Storm of the Century, one that then-weather watchers could not have predicted.

The newlyweds returned from their honeymoon and began married life in Joanna's house, along with Grandma and younger siblings. Three months later Walter was drafted into military service and, on July 23, 1951, he was sent to Korea. There was a war on, of course, and he was put into immediate action. Once on the front, Walter used his technical skills in directing a wire-laying team to maintain a network that would provide uninterrupted communications to the battalion.

On Mach 12, 1952, Walter voluntarily advanced to the front to repair damaged communications lines. Despite enemy shelling, he refused to seek the protection of nearby bunkers on his mission. While splicing the lines, he was mortally wounded by a burst of mortar fire.

Meanwhile, back in Bayonne, ever since Walter was sent overseas, Aunt Joanna devoted her Saturday afternoons to shopping for something or other for Walter. But on Saturday, March 22, 1952, she told her mother that she had no desire to leave the house that day and that she had a premonition. Earlier in the day, Aunt Joanna had read a letter from Walter several times over and was happy to learn that his communications work was miles behind the Korean line and far from danger.

My Dad's Aunt Joanna and Uncle Walter, circa 1951.

At 6:45 p.m., a telegram arrived from the U. S. Armed Forces notifying her that Walter had been killed in action on March 12. The day before, Walter had written that long letter telling Aunt Joanna of his duties and his location, as she had requested. While she was reading the letter from Walter, she was twenty-four hours from being notified he had been killed in battle. A letter from Washington soon confirmed the telegram.

In his last letter, Walter had told his wife of his activities. "Today I will answer your questions. You don't have to worry. I am confined to what is known as the Punch Bowl. I am about ten miles behind the lines. I sleep very comfortably and am very warm … I am a crew chief now—since my promotion to corporal, I often have twenty men assigned under me. Our duties are to provide communication lines and to make repairs when necessary—a troubleshooter. I have a good job and I like it. So you don't have to worry about me … Korea is a mass of hills—one picture shows all of Korea—nothing but hills and more hills …" Weeping, Aunt Joanna said to a news reporter who interviewed her following Walter's death, "He said 'don't worry…'"

My Mom's Uncle Lou and Aunt Helene
on their wedding day, 1952.

The Test

Mom's aunt Helene had met her husband, Uncle Lou, while on a visit to the Jersey shore with a friend, right around 1950. Lou was there with a couple of his friends, enjoying the beautiful day. It was a Saturday afternoon, and Helene had stopped into a local church to have her confession heard before Mass the next day. It was there that she noticed Lou in the back of the church. Later that day, she was introduced to him. Helene and Lou instantly hit it off, and had a great time that evening talking and dancing to the music of Vaughn Monroe. Meeting Helene made such an impact on him that, when the night was over, Lou announced to his buddies, "I'm gonna marry that girl!" True love did blossom and, once they knew that they were serious about each other, they felt it was time for Uncle Lou's parents to meet Helene. She very excitedly arranged to travel up to Massachusetts one weekend. In speaking to his parents about Helene, Lou had mentioned that he met her in a church. Years ago, some people used church as a slang word for bar, and before Lou could explain, his parents shared a sideways glance at each other.

It turns out that Uncle Lou's parents were thrilled to meet the girl who had stolen their son's heart. Sometime during that first visit, Lou's father decided he was going to very subtly test Helene's domestic abilities. He approached her with a problem. "Helene, maybe you can help me. I just had a button come off my shirt here. Could I trouble you to sew it back on if you have a minute?" Lou's mother was busy cooking at the time, but she produced a spool of white thread and a needle for her prospective daughter-in-law. That's how Helene knew she had the relationship all sewn up.

The Big Sister

Mom had two siblings. My uncle Nicky was fifteen and my aunt Susan was nine when Mom made her appearance in the early 1950s. Aunt Susan was very excited to take the drive to the hospital when it was time to take the new baby home. However, Susan's excitement was short lived, as the adorable little bundle in her arms (no mandatory safety seat in those days) left her with a very wet lap. So much for cloth diapers literally dampening spirits! It was the first of two incidents that had lifelong teasing consequences by big sister to little sister.

The second (and worse) one occurred when my mother was probably three or four years old. Aunt Susan had a pet bird, Chipper, that she absolutely loved. He was a beautiful shade of blue. He was kept in a cage in the kitchen and she very much enjoyed spending time talking to him and feeding him treats like an occasional celery leaf. He was a pet of her very own. Every once in a while, my grandmother would place the bird cage on their back porch to get some air and enjoy the outside while safely behind bars. My mom sometimes took that opportunity to sit next to the cage and hang out with little Chipper. One day, Chipper must have seemed a little sad to my mother. All around the back yard, the sound of happy birds could be heard in the spring air. Soooo, in her little three-year-old logic, little Marigene thought she could solve Chipper's loneliness. Bye, Bye, Birdie! Cage open, parakeet AWOL. The neighbors were probably left wondering what all the noise was about outside my mom's house for a while there.

As time went on, though, the two sisters became closer. Once she got her driver's license, Aunt Susan took my mom on rides in her second-hand car (back in the day you almost never got your own car at seventeen). Mom got used to hearing a lot of 1950s music on the radio as they rode. Or my aunt treated Mom to an ice cream cone while on a walk downtown, which was only a few blocks away from their house.

My mother and her siblings, Nicky and Sue.
Mom is in the middle, circa 1955.

A while after my grandmother passed away, Aunt Susan got married and started a family. But she always remained close to my mom in spirit. One of their favorite movies was (and still is) *The Wizard of Oz*. Aunt Susan still calls my mom on the phone whenever she sees that it's on TV or will be soon. The Wicked Witch is their favorite character. "Who killed my sister?? Was it you??"

The best part of being sisters developed over the past several years. Mom and Aunt Susan have always exchanged greeting cards for occasions, especially birthdays. Even better than being sisters by birth was the fact that Aunt Susan started referring to Mom as her best friend. That put things in a different light and is very much appreciated by Mom.

My mother, Marigene, on her First Communion Day.

The Special Delivery

Uncle Nicky has always been an avid fisherman, and one of mom's favorite childhood things to do was to watch how her brother produced all the worms he needed before he headed out to one of his best fishing spots. Mom would sit nearby as Nicky found little worm holes in the backyard lawn. He would mix mustard powder with water and slowly pour it into the holes. This was definitely not a cool thing for the worms, because it would drive them all up out of the dirt to escape the fumes and heat. But it got my uncle the supply of bait that he needed. On fishing day, that's all that mattered.

Among Mom's childhood photos, there is one from Christmas morning, maybe in 1958. Behind her in the scene is a framed photo of Nicky, proudly displayed by my grandmother on a table in their living room. He served in the U. S. Navy for four years, based in Connecticut on submarine duty. Between being in the service and then attending college, he wasn't always around the house for Mom to hang out with.

Around 1961, Mom was in second grade, and she was preparing at her Catholic grade school to make her first Communion. To a seven-year-old, this is an exciting time. It's when you learn all about how Jesus showed the apostles how to remember him, initiating the sacrament. Along with classroom instruction, girls would, and still do, shop for a white dress and a headpiece with a veil. Mom still has both of her own stored away. The whole family was excited for mom's upcoming

Communion experience, but at the time, my Uncle Nicky was in the service and not able to be home for the big day. His presence would be missed by all. Shortly before First Communion Day, there was a knock on the door at Mom's house. It was a delivery man with a long, white ribbon-topped box in his hands. Whomever answered the door was surprised, but even more impressed when the card attached to the box had Mom's name on it! My mother was summoned from playing with her dolls, and was completely amazed that this gift was for her alone! The box was taken to the kitchen table where, inside the folds of soft, green tissue paper were one dozen gorgeous, red roses. The note tucked inside read Congratulations on your first communion, Marigene. Love, Nicky

My uncle had made the day and a life-long memory for his little sister!

The Things We Do for Love

It was July 1961, and my mom's mother was suffering from terminal cancer. She was just shy of her forty-third birthday, and mom was eight years old. Mom did not know the extent of my grandmother's illness, as it was a difficult thing to explain to a kid, but she witnessed family members sponge bathing and feeding her as the illness worsened. There was a can of mentholated pain relief cream in their bathroom, but, being so young, mom did not understand its purpose.

There was an American history-themed amusement park in New York called Freedom Land, and in those days it was a hot spot for kids to visit. There were a lot of attractions to see and places to eat, and so on. My mom always said that her favorite was a reenactment of the Chicago Fire, where kids would help actors portraying firemen extinguish a controlled fire that went off every hour.

Some friends of our family decided to visit the park one weekend that July, and they invited my grandmother and mom to go along. Years later, Mom was with the daughter in that family when she produced a photograph she wanted Mom to have. It was of their little group in the parking lot before they entered the park. There are not a lot of photographs of my grandmother that exist, as she was on the shy side, but there she stood with Mom, the youngest of her three children, at her side. Grandma's hair had thinned out quite a lot following her cancer treatment, and her clothes were fitting somewhat looser, but she had been determined to give my mother an exciting day with our friends.

To this day, Mom cherishes the Freedom Land photo, as my grandmother passed away seven months later, on February 7, 1962.

My Mom and Grandma Mary, far left, pictured with a group of friends at Freedomland, 1961.

The Godfather

When my mother was growing up, in addition to her parents and siblings, two of her uncles lived in the house. Her uncle Ronny was chosen to be Mom's godfather, (he also agreed to be my godfather), and he always enjoyed looking after her and being there for her, as godparents do. In mom's generation, there were twenty-eight male cousins, but only seven females, so Uncle Ron particularly treasured all of his nieces. Mom fondly remembers going for rides in his convertible MG, playing opera music as they drove, and the house was always filled with Frank Sinatra songs when Ronny was around. Between Uncle Ron and my mom's brother, Nicky, Mom was also introduced to great comedies like *The Soupy Sales Show*, *The Three Stooges*, and *The Addams Family*.

When Mom was eight years old, her mom, who had been ill with cancer, passed away at home. Being ill proved to be a long, slow ordeal for my grandmother—she suffered for a year and a half. The night she passed away, she somehow found the energy to walk upstairs behind Mom and put her to bed. Mom never saw her again. The next morning, after Grandma's death was gently explained to Mom, she was curled up in a living room chair and Uncle Ronny came to sit beside her. He did his best to consoler her, as difficult a task as it was.

My mother just before "the attack"
by my godfather, Ronny LaSala.

The Christmas when Mom turned ten years old, our godfather bought Mom a bicycle, and he proudly displayed it near the tree for her to enjoy "from Santa." She was thrilled, of course, and in the springtime was raring to go out and enjoy her new wheels. She had also acquired a puppy over that winter, whom she named Pal. On one of her initial rides in her neighborhood, Pal scampered behind her. She was riding along down her street, when she chanced to check behind her to make sure Pal wasn't running out into traffic, when it happened. Her front tire hit a section of sidewalk which was upended due to tree roots. Poor Mom, more concerned about her dog than herself, ended up flying over the handlebars onto her face. Don't even know if a helmet would have saved the day even if she had worn one. Years ago, it wasn't the safety factor it is today. The fall cut open her chin, requiring stitches, but worse than that, it traumatized her two front teeth. Eventually she would require a tooth bridge wide enough to cover a large, upper section of her pearly whites. Uncle Ron was beside himself with regret over his bicycle purchase, but really, that's life and sometimes stuff happens.

Uncle Ronny was the last to be born of my mother's aunts and uncles on her father's side and, when he passed away at age sixty-seven, at his funeral mass he was described as the link between generations. *This was very true,* I thought. He was beloved by all in the family, especially us cousins. There will never be another Uncle Ronny.

My Great-Grandmother, Savanella "Susan"
LaSala, a.k.a "Ma", with my Mom, 1953.

That Nana of Hers

While my mom and her siblings were growing up, they and my grandparents had the advantage of living with Grandpa's mother. There hadn't been a baby in Mom's house in nine years, until her appearance in 1953. The photo on the left is of my mom and her grandma, who at the time was sixty years old. Women in the previous generation didn't wear spandex- type exercise clothing like many do today. Instead they tied on aprons to protect their house dresses from the day's work.

It was an Italian household, with mom referring to her grandma as Nana. Nana herself had emigrated from Italy as a child, and was a fourteen-year-old bride, married here in the states. She and Mom's grandfather had ten children, among them my grandfather, Anthony, and Nana's children also had large families. On her birthdays and holidays, the house filled up with deliveries of fresh flowers and other tributes of the love our extended family had for her. Every Sunday, Mom enjoyed the company of many of her cousins who came to eat a huge Italian dinner cooked up by Nana. Pasta and meatballs, as well as many of her other specialty dinners, were enjoyed around a big dining room table. The amazing part about those large family dinners was that there was no dishwasher. Plates and everything else that goes with them needed to be washed and dried by hand. That's when the women folk got together and tidied up the kitchen. It gave them all a chance to chat and catch up as they worked.

Nana took taking care of her family very seriously, but she also had her funny side. Once she was watching Alfred Hitchcock's movie, *The Birds*, and one of my aunts walked into the house with her children, my cousins, for a visit. There was Nana, sitting two feet from the living room TV, volume up high so she could hear it. The scene was when Tippi Hedrin starts fearfully walking up the stairs to the attic. All of a sudden, everyone in the house heard Nana yell out "Don't go up there, lady—that's where they're hiding!!!"

It was mom's Nana, my great-grandmother, who did her best to help bring up my grandmother, who passed away from cancer when she was forty-three years old. Nana made sure to get Mom up in the morning and made her a lunch to take to school every day. Mom's father remarried when Mom was fourteen and he moved to his new wife's house, but Mom was able to remain living with her Nana at her house through high school so as not to disrupt her schooling. My grandpa and his wife visited Mom's house each night for dinner and to catch up on the day. The new little family group was always well fed by Nana.

We all miss you, Nana, and if there's a kitchen in heaven, I'm sure you're in charge of the stove!

A Truly Good Man

My mother owes the second half of her name to her uncle Gene, her dad's brother. What a good-hearted, loving man he was! No sooner had he graduated from high school in 1943, then Uncle Gene persuaded his father (and, more impressively, his mother) to allow him to enlist in the service during World War II. Like most boys his age, he was chomping at the bit to join the ranks of the military and serve his country. Uncle Gene did his part and was among the troops engaged in the Battle of the Bulge. Mom's family was proud of him for performing his duties, and welcomed him back home with open arms after the war.

My mom's Aunt Dot and Uncle Gene LaSala.

Uncle Gene went on to attend and graduate from, Syracuse University, majoring in microbiology. He was hired by Hoffmann LaRoche, and worked there for many years. During his employment, he was the inventor of a food additive for cattle, named Lasalocid in his honor.

Uncle Gene was famous for keeping track of every single member of Mom's large Italian family and their birthdays. It was a fairly big job —he had nine brothers and sisters, plus the next generation, and so on! In addition, all of these cards were mailed with a little extra something included …

Uncle Gene didn't require much in the way of possessions. So friends and family members were stumped as to what to get him each Christmas. And that is why there were something like twenty cartons of Lucky Strike cigarettes under the tree with his name on them!

The family homestead was well taken care of with Uncle Gene doing what he loved to do—tending to the yard and gardens. There was a large vegetable garden, fruit trees, and even a compost pile he kept up on to ensure that all of the plants were well taken care of. Mom's uncle would take it upon himself to spend many hours on spring and summer nights watering, feeding, and weeding away. Every weekend, you could hear the familiar sound of his lawn mower humming around the yard. Mom remembers her uncle not coming in to eat until it was almost dark outside.

In his thirties, Uncle Gene met a woman named Dorothy while at work at Hoffman LaRoche, and she eventually became my mom's Aunt Dot. They went on to have three sons—the loves of his life. I think there is a very special relationship between children and relatively older parents. Icing on the cake, if you will.

Uncle Gene left us at the age of ninety-two. At his funeral, there was a military presence that usually attends a veteran's ceremony, and Taps was played. My mother and my aunt Susan stood holding onto each other, softly sobbing. My aunt whispered to my mother, "We had him the longest ..."

That afternoon, my mother was out on her deck, thinking about Uncle Gene, who had been such an influence on her. All of a sudden, her eyes were drawn to a lilac plant next to the deck. Mom had planted this bush about five years previous, and knew not to expect any budding for a while, until it really took hold. To her amazement, there at the top of the bush was a beautiful, fully-bloomed lavender flower! To this day, Mom feels that Uncle Gene was trying to ease her sadness.

The Double Dip

Years ago, my mom and I were invited to my cousin's bridal shower. It was an in-home party, and many of us friends and relatives were sitting in the living room, feasting on a veggie platter that had an amazing dip. It was an enjoyable afternoon.

Two weeks later, Mom went for a visit to my uncle's luncheonette. She noticed her aunt Grace sitting on a stool at the counter. Mom sat down beside her and greeted her with her usual kiss on the cheek. As her aunt finished taking a bite of her hamburger, she noticed Mom there and said, "You did something terrible!" Mom was raised in a good Catholic household where behavioral infractions usually produced a good amount of guilt. It was a mental slap in the face—was Mom now banished from happiness in the next life?

My mother braved the question, "What do you mean?"

Aunt Grace clued her in on the reason for her pent-up disgust. "Don't you remember when we were at the shower? They had that vegetable tray?"

Okay, Mom thought, *Was someone deceased because of me? I don't recall making any digestive noises at the time ... to what catastrophe is this woman referring?*

Aunt Grace continued, with a piercing stare, "Well, I noticed that you double dipped a carrot stick! Uh huh—you dipped in one end and then just flipped that thing around and dipped in the other end!"

Oh Lord, save me. As the magnitude of her disappointment sunk in, Mom told me that she felt tears welling up, and she knew that ordering any lunch right then for herself would be pointless. She is one of those people who starve rather than gorge when traumatized. "No thanks, Paul," she said to the man who was behind the counter cooking. "Nothing for me. Just came to say hello." Sniff, sniff. Aunt Grace never had children of her own, but she always meant well, and always looked out for her many nieces and nephews.

That night about eight o'clock, Mom's phone rang. It was Aunt Grace. "Hey, I'm sorry I made you cry today. Why didn't you just tell me to go screw myself? You know that's just me sometimes!"

Mom knew that, deep down, Aunt Grace loved her, but my mother couldn't bring herself to tell her off, least of all to her face. To this day, Mom and I just smile at each other whenever we come across a tray of veggies and dip at someone's party.

*Pictured left to right, the LaSala girls, circa
1950s, Helene, Josie, "Ma", and Grace.*

The Beaded Purse

My mother had an Aunt Grace (on the far right), who once received a gorgeous clutch bag from her husband, Arnold. He had brought it back as a gift for her from France, where he served in World War II. The purse was intricately beaded on the outside, and Aunt Grace treasured it. She kept it for many years, and then one day she realized that she no longer used the purse very often and wanted to find someone else who might enjoy it as much as she had.

Meanwhile, one of my mother's cousins had married a woman by the name of Michelle, and when Grace and Arnold met Michelle, they were both struck by her resemblance to Grace as a young woman. They began calling Michelle "Young Grace." Then Aunt Grace began calling herself "Old Grace." One day when they were visiting, Michelle mentioned to Aunt Grace that she occasionally enjoyed selling things on the Internet and that she had had some success at it. Aunt Grace asked her if she wouldn't mind trying to find a buyer for her purse. Grace suggested that Michelle try to get around $100 for the purse, as it was such a beautiful, handmade item.

Michelle checked out similar clutch bags online, but what she discovered was that most, by that time, sold for only about ten or twenty dollars each. So, not wanting to disappoint Grace, Michelle kept the purse in her possession for a little while, and then did something "Graceful" for our aunt. Michelle decided that the kindest thing to do would be to mail Aunt Grace a personal check for $100 and tell her that the purse had actually sold online. Of course, Grace was thrilled to receive the payment.

Fast forward several years, when our family attended a burial service one day when Aunt Grace and Uncle Arnold's ashes were interred. At the conclusion, as Mom was talking to Michelle, the purse she had with her caught my Mom's eye, and that's when she told Mom its story. Michelle had thought to honor Grace by bringing the purse to her service and, in homage to our aunt, Young Grace continues to use the purse, but only for formal occasions. Michelle's sending payment to Aunt Grace regarding the purse sale has been the classiest use of a little white lie that my mother had ever run across.

The Mentor

Mary Jean and Nick Wood, circa 1970s.

In the late 1960s, my mom was part of a group of singers and musicians in her church. This was when guitar (folk) music was popular. It's also how she first met my dad. Several of Mom's cousins and many teens from surrounding towns were part of the group. The members got together every Friday night to practice and then perform the songs in church on Sundays. They also had use of an event room in the basement of the church and, on

Saturday nights, they hosted a coffee house where people could go and hear songs being played to guitar music.

The director of music was Mr. Nick Wood. He and his wife, Mary Jean, had a large family and lived in town. The Woods were very devoted to each other and to their growing family. They both enjoyed playing musical instruments and passed on that love to their children. Organ and guitar music were often heard throughout the house, mixed with the sounds of a loving, busy home life. Many times the choir members visited the Wood's home to go over new songs and just enjoy being with the family.

Mr. Wood took on the job of the church's choir director, but he proved to mean so much more to Mom and the entire group. The late 1960s and 1970s was a very trying time in our country, especially to kids in their teen years. The Vietnam War was dragging on and there was a lot of general unrest. However, Mr. Wood was always willing to lend an ear. Not all of the choir members had a stable family life, but Mr. Wood always made every one of them feel appreciated, and was genuinely concerned for their wellbeing.

Unfortunately, Mr. Wood passed away when he was only sixty-four, but his legacy of devotion to his family and his church will always be fondly remembered.

Always a Parent

I recently overheard someone I know sadly remark, "I miss my kids—they aren't around anymore …" It was because his children were grown and out of the house. One had gotten married and the other was miles away at college.

My grandfather, Nick LaSala, seated at the counter at "LaSala's – We Have Everything!"

I've heard my mother say that, over the course of the twenty or so years that a parent raises a child, the family is busily involved in what it takes to bring up their kids—getting them ready for school, going to work, driving them where they have to go, and so on. The list goes on. Then the day comes where they go off to college or move out of the house, and that happens before you know what hit you, Mom said.

I never knew my dad's father, Grandpa Al. He passed away even before my parents met. But I do have personal memories of my mom's father, Grandpa Nick. In the evenings and on weekends, he worked in my cousin's luncheonette, which was located on the corner of a very busy three-way intersection not too far from where we lived. One day Mom went to visit Grandpa at the store, and she needed to cross the street to buy something. Grandpa was about to cook some burgers for his customers but, instead, having heard my mom's plan, he came out from behind the counter because he saw her heading out of the store. They went outside together and he reached for her hand as they watched for an opening in the crazy traffic. Grandpa did not let go until Mom had reached the other side of the street. Once a parent, always a parent.

Channeling Grandpa

Grandpa Nick. A while back, the world lost a sweet, caring man. But, as the saying goes, if I have become my mother, it seems I have also become my grandfather! Perhaps he was watching over me as I began life in my first apartment. I found myself texting my mother about things I was doing in the kitchen that Grandpa had a habit of doing, like putting a paper clip on a bag of croutons to keep them fresh. Grandpa, of course, was from the pre-Tupperware age where you had to use any and all means available in the fight against staleness.

My grandparents, Mary and Nick LaSala, with my Mom's cousin Alice at her christening.

Another humorous text to Mom was when I used a rubber band around my plastic lunch container so that the top would not come off. Or when I covered a can of soda with tin foil before refrigerating it until the next day. These methods work well, but the most important thing is that Grandpa, someone whom I loved so much, always comes to mind and brings a smile to my face.

The photo that accompanies this story is a photo of Grandpa Nick and Grandma Mary from when they proudly served as godparents for my mom's cousin.

The Quotes

Grandpa Nick had some words to live by in his time. Bits of wisdom which, if not included in the pages of *Airport Socks*, would be a crime.

1. French fries—you gotta eat 'em while they're hot.

2. If credit card companies waited for me to use one, they'd go out of business.

3. Asparagus—if you don't buy them on sale, it's highway robbery.

4. When you are sitting at a slot machine in a casino, always feed in the max amount of quarters each time.

5. If something went wrong or there was a disappointment, he would say "Piss on it!"

The Phone List

My grandfather (Mom's dad) kept friends' phone numbers on a page from a yellow legal pad. He referred to that page for years. The man lived to be ninety-one, so this list had tons of people on it when I first got a glimpse of it. In the pre-cell phone age where you could not store this type of information electronically, his paper roster proved invaluable.

One day, on a visit to Grandpa's house, I noticed that the list had some crossed-out names and their respective phone numbers. I did not want to ask Grandpa directly, so I mentioned it on the phone to my aunt shortly after the visit. She revealed something that was both sweet and, at the same time, sad. The crossed-out names were those who were now deceased. I mentioned this fact to my mother that day and we thought about how many names it actually came to. Her dad, who had had quite a full life at that point, had sadly outlived a lot of his acquaintances.

Several months later, Mom and Dad went to visit mom's Uncle Gene, who was Grandpa's younger brother, then in his eighties. She and Dad shot each other a glance, because, right there in Uncle Gene's kitchen near the wall phone, was a yellow legal pad with names on it, some of which were crossed out. A chronicle of time and friendship.

The Twelve-Hour Coffee

The other day I was at my parents' house. Mom asked if I wanted some coffee. She had a nice selection of coffee pods, so in thirty seconds I sat down to a nice steamy hot cup.

Mom looked at me wistfully and said, "Hey, remember Sunday night coffee at Grandpa's house?" My grandfather (Mom's dad) had an aluminum coffee pot on his kitchen counter years ago when my brother and I were kids. Grandpa was in his eighties back then, and every morning around 6:30 he would brew up a batch and whatever he didn't finish would remain in the pot the entire day.

While my brother and I were growing up, every Sunday evening our family would go to visit Grandpa, bringing along a fast-food dinner. The four of us were very close to my grandfather, and we looked forward to those weekend visits, a chance to catch up on each other's comings and goings.

After dinner and some TV viewing together, Grandpa warmed up the morning coffee and Mom and Dad had a cup along with whatever dessert we had brought. Of course, Mom told me that they always had antacid tablets ready later on, but they drank Grandpa's daily coffee out of love.

My grandfather, Nick LaSala, feeding his deer visitors.
(Painting by Nick's nephew, James R. LaSala,
New Mexico, circa 1990s)

The Gentleman in the First Car

My mother is an avid biography reader, and she at one time picked up a book written by Marlo Thomas. Marlo said that her father, the actor Danny Thomas, once told a joke about a funeral procession going by. A man noticing the line of cars asked the cop on the corner, "Who died?" The cop replied, "The gentleman in the first car."

That story reminded me of my grandfather, Anthony, whom everyone called Nick. Grandpa meant the world to me, as well as to all the other members of my family. He left us at the age of ninety-one, but there was so much of his personality that he left for us. He was the most compassionate person I ever knew. He was one of ten siblings from an Italian couple right off the boat.

Grandpa Nick worked in his brother's luncheonette through all of the years of my childhood. On Saturday at lunchtime, my parents drove us over to the store to eat and spend some time near Grandpa, who was in his glory flipping burgers and patting down grilled cheese sandwiches. A very sociable man, he was in his element whenever he was at work.

Grandpa's youngest brother, my godfather, had some low periods in his life, and Grandpa's door was always open to him. On Sunday nights, we visited Grandpa, who lived alone following the death of his second wife (my mom's stepmother). Occasionally, my godfather would stop by and join us for coffee and great conversation.

My grandfather was a great nature lover. His house had a very wooded backyard and, for years, there was a herd of about a dozen deer that would come to the backyard and he happily fed them. Several times a day he scooped a container of cracked corn from a small barrel outside his house and poured it along the edge of his driveway, and then enjoyed a visit from his deer. It's no wonder that my mom has always fed the birds in our backyard—it's in her genes!

When Grandpa was eighty-nine years old, he developed a leg infection that caused him to require amputation surgery. At the time he was a resident of a nursing home in the area, his house and most of his belongings having been sold. When that occurs in a person's life, they have a good chance of becoming bitter and turning off from the world. Not Grandpa—he adapted remarkably well to life in the home, and we made sure to visit him regularly, as did several of his friends. About a year and a half later, Grandpa developed an infection common to senior citizens in hospitals—one that was incurable—and it caused his death.

When death occurs to family or friends, and you are in the line of cars headed to the cemetery to bury the person, a very powerful ritual takes place in our area. The funeral line will very slowly and reverently pass by the house and through the neighborhood where the deceased person lived, and that is what happened in Grandpa's case. A bittersweet tribute to this man in the first car.

The Surprise Visit

In the early 1980s, there was a family that my parents were friends with that lived nearby. The neighbor couple had a daughter who was right around my brother's age. At the time, I was just an infant and my brother was three. As Christmas was approaching that year, the thought was that it might be fun if Santa Claus could make an appearance for the kids. The other couple offered to have a small celebration at their house, and my father consented to play the part of the man in the red suit.

My brother AJ with "Santa", 1980s.

On party day, we were all assembled at the neighbor's house amid their Christmas tree and all the beautiful decorations. The adults were all sitting around enjoying the holiday food, with the kids busy playing on the floor. After a while, we all heard the sound of jingling bells coming from outside. The kids looked up from their toys in wonder at what it could be. All of a sudden, the doorbell rang and our neighbor proceeded to answer it. "Who could it be?" wondered the fascinated children. None other than Santa Claus came bounding up the steps into the living room, with a bulging bag flung across his shoulder! "Merry Christmas everyone! Ho, Ho, Ho!"

The children could not believe their eyes! They were amazed beyond words. Santa seated himself on the chair he was hurriedly provided with, and my brother was the first one to sit on the big man's lap. Expecting to hear all of the goodies on my brother's Christmas list, Santa was, instead, startled to hear him say, "Santa! You have shoes just like my daddy!"

The Lost Tooth

Soon after my brother was born, my father, who had been over-weight for years, decided that it was time he got into better shape. He began paying closer attention to what he ate and he also began a program of running for exercise. He started to feel much better before too long, and he also grew to enjoy the running so much that be entered long-distance races. He even ran a few full-length marathons in those days.

When I was about five years old, Dad entered a race that was going to take place in Lancaster, Pennsylvania. Rather than rent a hotel room for the four of us, there was a discount deal for the runners to rent a cabin and have kind of a rustic little vacation. It sounded like a very exciting adventure, mostly in the mind of my brother, who was all set for a cool weekend in the wild. I, myself, was not quite sure about that.

Once we arrived at the campground, it became apparent that I was not going to enjoy myself. The Holiday Inn was a far cry from our cabin—the only items inside were mattresses and a broom. Even at five years old, I was thinking, *Check please!* However, the four of us soon settled down and I made the best of it. After a while, we decided to have a look around the wooded campgrounds. Mom and I found the ladies room, and that was my second surprise of the day—a communal shower area. I had never seen one of those before, and I knew right then that, until it was time to leave, I'd be washing my face and brushing my teeth, but that's as far as modesty would take me on this trip!

Now for the part of the weekend that I marveled about for a long time—when we left on our trip, I had my first loose tooth. The day after we arrived it had worked itself out, and then—my fear set in—how would the Tooth Fairy ever find me here in the middle of Pennsylvania? After all, I hadn't left a note or directions! Mom saw how worried I was and she took the time to comfort me. Apparently it was common knowledge that the Tooth Fairy never misses her mark.

Me with Mr. Pinkerton, Early 2000s

The next morning when I woke up, I was both excited and fearful. Dare I check under my pillow that I had brought from home? Ever so slowly, I slid my hand underneath and … there was my quarter! The going rate has gone up since, but to me at that moment, all was right with my world.

Today's Special

When I was very young, in the 1980s, there was a children's program called *Today's Special*. It was on every weekday afternoon when my brother and I got home from school, and we watched it faithfully. It was set in a department store, and it dealt with employees of the store, including a mannequin that came to life at night to interact with the others.

Grammy kept a faithful eye on the both of us until our parents got home from work. She had an afternoon routine where she watched two soaps without fail. That is, until my brother and I got old enough that we had developed an interest in *Today's Special*. That was back in the day when many families had only one TV in the house. It wasn't long before Grammy began to sacrifice half of her second soap, but in a very gracious way—she came to enjoy watching her grandchildren's eyes light up when their favorite show came on, and they could relax with her for a while after school. Grammy's gesture so long ago taught me about giving a little of yourself, out of love.

My grandmother, Victoria Kowalski, circa 1940s.

The Food Bypass

My paternal grandmother, Victoria, whom my brother and I called Grammy, had survived the Great Depression with her six siblings, and it was an especially hard time for the family, which didn't have much money in the first place. They lived on one floor of a two-story house that only had two official bedrooms, so makeshift beds appeared in every room except the kitchen.

Their hardship did produce one good habit, and it was that she and her siblings were taught to always finish whatever food supply had already been in the house or ice box (a primitive method of refrigeration) before beginning a new one. We were taught that good, economical rule of thumb from an early age.

The Story of "Eau"

When I was a little girl and I got thirsty, Mom was always there to give me a glass of water out of the tap. That came complete with a smile and a "How's my girl doing?" I got refreshment and a moment to bond with my mother. As I got older, I began getting my own water out of the tap, no matter who was around. Same refreshment, but with the addition of ice.

Then came the technology of water in a bottle: Handy concept and lots of money to be made, but not exactly the best for the environment.

Move ahead in the time line to the 2000s and along comes enhanced water, with the magic of added vitamins. And an even higher price tag.

These days, I am a filtered water-pitcher fan, and the "How's my girl doing?" is as close as my cell phone.

Boots the Cat, or When They Gave Out Patience, I was in the Ladies Room

When my brother and I were in grade school, my family had a female cat named Patches. We did have two females at one time, but the other had passed on. Missing the second cat, I nagged my mother relentlessly to get another. Finally, Mom broke down. When the local paper came, we checked the ads for pets to adopt, and we found one named Boots that seemed to fit the bill.

I was one excited kid the day we arranged for Boots to be brought to our house by her owner. The man was happy that we were giving Boots a new home, as his fiancée found that she was allergic to the poor cat. It was suggested that we give Boots a couple of days with our own cat so that they could get used to each other. The man took Boots out of her carrier and let her sniff around and check out her new digs. So far, so good. Of course, she hadn't met Patches yet. That didn't happen until about an hour later—the two cats discovered each other and all hell broke loose. So began a feline cat stare-down—and chase! Next thing everyone knew, I was crying and screaming, "Get that cat out of here. She's going to kill Patches! Oh my God!"

Mom and Dad didn't have to lift a finger. Patches was smart enough to get the heck out of there before she even knew what had happened in the first place. Boots ran in the opposite direction, and we didn't hear a peep out of either cat for hours.

Before long, it was bedtime on the first day. We figured (or hoped) that maybe overnight, the two cats would investigate each other without too much more fur flying. When our family woke up the next morning, there was absolutely no sign of Boots whatsoever. Like, in a scary way. From the top floor of the house to the cellar—nothing. No meows, no cat peeking out from anywhere. After a long search of every possible cubbyhole we could think of, we figured that somehow Boots had just escaped from the house and was out o' here. Mom and Dad left for work and my brother and I got on the school bus. Grammy, who was home during the daytime, had a routine of watching a couple of soaps, and this day was no different. In those days, my parents had a wooden cabinet in the TV room where they kept an old-fashioned record player. The back of this cabinet was hollowed out to fit the stereo and their collection of vinyl record albums. Grammy was relaxing and watching TV when, suddenly, she heard a noise coming from the cabinet. Thinking she was imagining things, she shrugged it off at first. But then the noise began to sound more like the meows of a cat, and the jig was up. She had discovered Boots' hideout—any port in a storm, it seemed! I don't know who was more spooked at that point, Grammy or Boots! The cat didn't move from that spot—all curled up inside the cabinet, fearing for her life—and Grammy was definitely not going to fish out a cat with attitude.

Even when Mom and Dad got back home, they found it impossible to get to Boots to remove herself from her hiding place. It would have taken a pair of hawk gloves! Dad had to contact the original owner and request that he return for his cat. The things I put my father through...

The Service Project

My brother and I had been enrolled in religious education classes at our church since first grade. Our mom served as a volunteer teacher for my grade in 1991, the year I turned ten. Operation Desert Storm was ramping up, so we sent letters and personal items to the military through our local newspaper. We thanked the service people for their efforts and hoped that they would find some solace in our mass communication effort.

Time went by, and one day in 2012 my mother received a large white envelope in the mail. The return address was San Antonio, Texas. Mom thought, *Is this what I think it is? After all these years!* Our particular letter was received by a man named Jose who was stationed in Saudi Arabia as a medic. He enclosed a photo of himself in uniform from back in the day. It seems that when his tour of duty ended, he took home with him a duffel bag of 500 letters like ours. He made a promise to himself during Desert Storm that, no matter how long it took, he would answer each one of them, and include a photo, so that every family would know to whom they had sent a letter. The last line of his letter to us mentioned that he never forgot us and thanked us for our support all those years.

Our Desert Storm Pen Pal, Jose, 1990s.

Sadly, not long after Jose had received the package from my classroom, he was injured during a night bombing, affecting the right side of his body. His injuries required surgery and intensive physical therapy. He was determined to connect with and acknowledge everyone who had reached out to him. In his second letter to us, Jose mentioned that he was on duty that night and, about half an hour later, when he was through treating patients, he opened our letter. He said that it felt good to see the faces of Americans after so long.

My mom was so excited to receive this mail after two decades had gone by, that she contacted our local newspaper, which printed an article about our good fortune.

In future letters to Jose, Mom shared various family doings, such as my wedding, my brother's wedding, and the birth of my son. Jose mentioned that he had a hand in the raising of his niece, and that her wedding was one of the proudest moments of his life.

Mom has made a tradition of baking cookies for Jose as a birthday gift each year and, periodically, he has been kind enough to mail a batch of beautiful home-made greeting cards for my family's use. Mom and Dad are always happy to receive a call from Jose with Christmas wishes for all of us. Jose has mentioned that he has joined a local gym and has healed enough that he began participating in run/walk races, with the help of his walker—which is no longer necessary—or hiking poles. As further healing took place, hiking and camping have also restored his self confidence.

Of all the years she taught religious education, my mother looks back with the most heart-felt satisfaction on the connection that the class achieved with those military members in need of a word or two from back home.

In His Name

My parents once volunteered at their church to spend an evening helping homeless families. The church houses these families for one week each year during the summer, and people sign up to donate food or time—or both—to the cause. The program is called In His Name, referring to the compassion of Jesus.

When Mom and Dad arrived to help out, they initially felt a bit awkward as one might expect, but not for long. The hospitality team had their welcoming act completely together and were in the process of serving dinner. Mom was asked to assist with the inflation of a few air mattresses and, on her way to one of the rooms used for sleep, she came upon two adorable little girls on their way to dinner with their dad. These girls were wearing cute little hand-me-down dresses and had big smiles on their faces. You could see that they were just happy to be in the company of people who cared about their welfare. After dinner, the children were delighted to have volunteers interacting, with donated toys for them. When you are little kids, you have no idea about financial and social problems in life, as long as there is a loving atmosphere in the family, even if you are constantly being shifted from one place to another to survive.

I spoke to my mother the next day, and she mentioned the experience at church. Our own family did not take big vacations every year and insist on designer clothing, and so on, but my brother and I felt that we had all we needed for our well-being. Mom said that it really puts your priorities in line when you can drive back home to the house that you own and really be grateful for it.

The Brownie Tray

One Saturday during my junior year of high school, my parents signed up to assist on a project run by our church. Once a month, anyone interested in volunteering could assemble in the parking lot and be driven by bus to a church hall a few towns over. There they would assist in preparing and serving a breakfast for food-insecure people. The food is normally donated by parishioners of our church and then brought over on the bus with us. I have to admit that I was a bit skeptical at first, never having done anything like that for a group of people I had never met. But, in the end, I signed myself on to give it a try. Turns out I became so full of anticipation as the day drew nearer, that I decided to take it upon myself to bake a tray of brownies to bring along.

It was about a half-hour bus ride for us volunteers and our bounty, and it was actually kind of exciting and intriguing at the same time. When we arrived at the church hall, we volunteers filed into the church kitchen to begin preparing the various foods that we had brought with us. There were eggs, bacon, bread, and fruit, as well as coffee and juice for everyone. In about a half hour or so, everything was ready to serve, and the kitchen smelled amazing!

What happened next really made an impression on me— all of the workers left the kitchen for a minute and assembled in the cafeteria to be with these needy folks in order to say a prayer of thanksgiving. We all stood in the area in front of the tables and formed a ring, holding hands. A grace before meals was said, and it made me realize that we are really one big family of people, some more fortunate than others.

Following the prayer, we helpers filed back into the church kitchen, ready to serve up our steaming-hot breakfast. As we spooned out each item, the gazes of many humble people met our eyes, people who were grateful for this breakfast. It was evident that our guests were truly appreciative of our efforts that morning.

My tray of brownies was placed at the end of the food line, where I happened to be standing. Following the breakfast service, a small group of young boys approached the tray in total amazement, with dropped jaws. The idea that someone would bother to make a yummy dessert available for the taking was almost beyond their belief! It was the same look as if they had come downstairs on Christmas morning and seen a bicycle with each boy's name on it. It was a moment that I don't think I'll ever forget. A simple service project produced such warm feelings all around! It was all the inspiration I needed to continue doing even simple good deeds going forward.

The Meatball—A Love Story

My mother has a good friend who shared a story with my mom about when she was a newlywed.

This friend, Theresa, was going to be hosting her husband John's parents and grandparents for dinner one Sunday. Being Italian, naturally there was spaghetti and meatballs on the menu. Not much of a stretch. So Theresa set about planning and shopping for what she needed, all the while very excited about her chance to impress her new family. That Sunday morning, she and her husband made sure the apartment was all in order, and Theresa started in with her cooking. She was using the meatball recipe that had been handed down from her mother who, in turn, had handed it down from her mother. It was going to be a great afternoon!

Before she knew it, the doorbell was ringing and Theresa's little dog barked excitedly, running to greet the visitors. Theresa was greeted at the door by John's family members, who had brought a beautiful bouquet of flowers along with them.

They all enjoyed a wonderful afternoon at the dinner table, with Theresa feeling more and more relaxed as the day wore on. It was apparent that this initial attempt at showing off her cooking skills had been a success, and she was very happy.

Later that night, while Theresa and her husband were in the living room after the family had left, John told her that he wanted to show her something. He opened up his hand, and in his palm was an adhesive bandage. Earlier that afternoon, it seemed that Theresa had cut her finger and apparently, while preparing her meatballs, the bandage had fallen into the mix. Fortunately, it was her husband who happened to choose the meatball with the surprise inside! He had lovingly chosen to wait until a quiet moment at the end of the day to reveal that to her. Good husband.

The Accident

Throughout my high school years, I was babysitter for the family across the street. They have six children—five girls and one boy—so it was quite a convenient arrangement and was the source of a little extra income for me.

One nice spring day after school, when I went across the street to watch the kids, Jennifer, the mom, was getting ready for work. Her son, John, called out to her, "Hey mom, can I ride my bike to Danny's house in a while?"

Jennifer called back to him, "O–kay, but make sure you wear your helmet!" About a half hour later, John put on his helmet, hopped on his bike, and left the house on his way to visit Danny, who lived a couple of blocks away on a street that had a twenty-five-mile-per-hour speed limit. Riding along, enjoying the beautiful weather, John felt like he didn't have a care in the world as he flew down the road to his friend's house. Before too long, he heard the distinct roar of a car behind him—one that sounded like it was doing a lot more than twenty-five miles per hour! Danny's street is notorious for speeders. It's a couple of miles long, and that makes it tempting for drivers who have the urge to wind out their engines upward of much higher speeds. As the car got closer, John suddenly had a terrible feeling, like there was no way he could pedal fast enough to avoid any oncoming trouble. Closer and closer came the engine sound until—Bam! —John was propelled off the bicycle.

John was lying unconscious in the roadway, his helmet and one shoe knocked off by the impact. The driver of the car happened to be a young town resident. Fortunately, he stayed on the scene. Anyway, his windshield had shattered when John had been tossed into it by the force of the crash. I should mention that this was prior to the age of cell phones, so the driver was forced to approach a nearby house to contact the local police. It happened very close to Danny's house, and his father came running out to find that it was an accident involving John. He contacted me while I was holding down the fort with John's sisters, and I placed a call to Jennifer at her job to give her the bad news. My grandmother lived with us in the house across the street, so I brought the girls over so that she could keep an eye on them while I rushed to the accident scene. It was amazing how expertly she handled the incoming accident-related calls while keeping an eye on all five of John's sisters! I located Jennifer's address book at their house in case I needed any contact information for the police and brought that with me, as I rode to the hospital with Danny's father. Turns out John had suffered a broken leg and bruises, and—more importantly—head trauma, so he was airlifted to a local hospital. The medevac team used the parking lot of the local elementary school as a landing pad, and safely delivered John to the hospital's emergency entrance. Fortunately, John did not have any life-threatening injuries, but he was hospitalized for a couple of days for care and observation. In the days following the accident, it seemed like the entire town came together with gifts and cards in support of John and his family.

I was glad to have been of assistance on that day, but even more glad that Jennifer was the one who had given John her permission to take that ride!

The Gadget Drawer Revealed

The kitchen everything drawer. Mom, what the hell?

Scene: Our kitchen during my college years, where Mom is preparing a holiday dinner. She, of course, asked me to help her prepare stuff, and I was rooting around in her vast utensil drawer, where there are all kinds of gadgets. I had no idea what many of them were for. "Mom, when was the last time you cleaned this drawer out? How old was I the last time you used any of this, I mean really?"

Mom, by this time in full-on holiday-busy mode, stopped just long enough to give me a sideways glance. It said, *You'll see!* Here is what ensued and, amazingly, how it has made me a better, gadget-loving person.

Mom said, "Do me a favor. Fill up the olive oil bottle on the counter." So I pulled out the gallon-size metal oil can, took off the top, and hoisted the damn thing up so I could pour out of it. Of course, I proceeded to get more on the counter than into the bottle. Not good. In a flash, my mother stopped mid-stir and opened up the gadget drawer. "You're gonna need this!" She pulled out the little funnel that should have made my life easier with an oil pour. Lesson one.

A little while later, she asked me to make sure some of the drippings from the turkey got into the bird as it was cooking. So I grabbed a fork and made some holes all over the top of the bird. Next thing I knew, I heard, "What on earth are you doing to that turkey??" Once again she pulled open the drawer, this time to find her turkey injector kit, which looked like it belonged in a medical office. It was a plastic box with three pieces in it that, when assembled, apparently sucked up the pan drippings so that I could poke a little hole and inject them directly into the bird with no visible markings. Uh huh. Lesson two.

"Honey, why don't you just go into the other room and find something on TV. I'll be fine with all this, really!" Mom wiped her brow because she obviously won't be, but she's at the end of her rope.

"No it's okay," I told her.

"Look, why don't you work on the other side of the kitchen, maybe on dessert?" That sounded like a plan, and how badly could I screw up on fruit? Right. I took half of a watermelon out of the fridge and placed it on the counter. I figured the cheese slicer would probably work to produce enough melon shavings to throw into a fruit salad. So I went over on the other side, and Mom, the inspector, took a three-second break from her work. "Sweetheart, didn't you check out the drawer for the melon baller? Come over here with me. I'll show you."

Do I really feel her guiding my arm? And there I was introduced to an instrument with two cup-like silver things, one on each end, which proved itself to work much better than the cheese slicer for getting watermelon ready for the fruit salad. Lesson three, and a plan to stock up on the household gadgets I never knew existed.

Cinnamon or Paprika? The Spice Industry's Little Joke

When I was a teenager watching my mother cook, I noticed that she always kept the cinnamon container and the paprika container on different shelves of our kitchen spice rack. On purpose, it seemed. I heard about it if I screwed up and accidentally placed them near each other when helping her clean up. It never occurred to me to ask her why.

One day when I had my first serious boyfriend, his mom and dad made plans to host a family picnic. I decided that it might be nice to impress everyone by showing them how well my mother had taught me to make macaroni salad. I envisioned Vinny's grandpa saying, "Hey, you hang on to this girl. She's a keeper! Great salad!"

I shopped for all of the ingredients, rolling down the supermarket aisles on a mission. My quest took me on the lookout for the freshest celery, most-expensive pasta, the best-looking onion in the bin. I even went for broke with a brand new mayo jar. The only thing I would not need to buy was the paprika that I would sprinkle over the salad once I had brought it to perfection.

Back at the house, the time had arrived to create my masterpiece. Got the pasta pot out, timed the cooking for just the right amount of minutes, and chopped up my celery and onion nice and tiny. I even hard-boiled a couple of eggs to slice on top, as my mother always did.

When I arrived at the picnic, I saw that Vinny's mom had set aside a special spot for me to place my salad bowl. I was feeling the love.

The burgers and dogs were ready before too long, and I felt very excited, hoping for some compliments on my trial run. Everyone came to heap up their plates, especially Vinny's grandpa, with a twinkle in his eye.

After a few minutes of munching pleasure on that gorgeous sunny afternoon, I began to sense that something was amiss. I started hearing, "Who made the macaroni salad?" So, naturally, I raised my hand, and then I thought it would be cute if I stood up and took a bow. *Here it comes,* I thought. *Thanks, Mom, for teaching me how to make a great side dish!* Surely grandpa was in salad heaven—there was no doubt in my mind. Or was he?

I turned toward where he was sitting, and then I heard it, "Why the hell is there cinnamon in this macaroni salad??"

The Ever-Handy Arrow

I am a very tidy person, and always keep my house neat. Actually, obsessively neat would describe how I operate, except for the cat in my life.

When I was in college and living at home, my parents got a cat, so Pinky was around the house for quite some time before I moved out. Whenever the cat ate something that didn't agree with him, he would, without fail, hack it up on the nearest carpet. It's part of a cat's standard operating procedure that pisses the owner off.

One day, several months after I had moved out, I stopped at my parents' house really quickly when no one was home, and I noticed that the cat had once again picked out a nice spot on the rug to lose his lunch. As I was in a rush, I found a slip of paper and drew an arrow on it. I placed it on the carpet so it pointed to the puke. I haven't lived that one down yet.

The Punch Bowl

One winter, while I was helping my mother clean out a closet, I noticed a large, square box that I had never paid particular attention to before. It contained a very carefully wrapped punch bowl, and there was a collection of matching glasses included. I said, "Ma, what's the deal? I never knew we had a punch bowl. It's gorgeous!"

She replied, "Yeah, it's been in the family for a long time. It was your great-grandmother's. I knew it was stored away, I guess I just never bothered to check it out."

Now, I had a challenge! My friends would just love this. I began searching the Internet for punch recipes. Most of them were for cold drink mixtures but, on one site they gave some hot punch recipes and one of them sounded delicious: wassail, a type of apple cider. It made me envision a freezing cold winter evening with friends gathered around our fireplace, munching on all kinds of goodies. It could be a bring-your-own night, whatever each girl's specialty was, and it could be washed down with this wonderful, warm cider. A great opportunity to display and enjoy that antique crystal!

I phoned a bunch of friends, and most of them were available for the following Saturday night. Mom and Dad were going to the movies anyway, so we ladies had the place to ourselves. I only wished I had come upon that punch bowl set much sooner. I was thinking of what a great party this was going to be.

On Saturday, after greeting everyone and making sure they were comfortable with drinks and appetizers, I brought out the punch set and got all the ingredients ready for my cider. Before long, the wonderful, heady scent of the apples and spices filled the air, as the mixture began gently bubbling. What an amazing centerpiece it would make! My friends could not get over how beautiful and unique the whole set was. I told them its history, and that I couldn't wait for the opportunity to use it that night.

When the cider was ready, in about half an hour, everyone gathered around the bowl. I carried the cider pot carefully over to the bowl and gently poured in the gallon of delicious brew. Proudly looking around the gathered circle of my friends, I imagined my great-grandmother lovingly looking down on the scene. But in the next moment, there came what sounded like a crackling noise. Gentle at first, and then gradually louder. What was happening on the serving table?

Before anyone realized it, my friends and I watched helplessly as the entire punch bowl slowly cracked in half and gave way! Cascades of hot brown liquid began to pool at our feet. It was one of those *Am I really seeing this?* moments. It wasn't until the next day that I noticed a note in the box that held the punch bowl. It was in what was probably great-grandma's handwriting, and it said, "Always remember to place a metal spoon in the bowl before you pour in the punch, so that the bowl can slowly adjust to the heat."

The Extra Button

When I was just a few months old and my brother was three, our family moved in with our widowed paternal grandmother. It took some adjustment for all of us but, before long, we realized the benefits that an extended family can offer. As a result of our family merger, my brother and I grew very close to our grandmother over the years. My mother was able to work various jobs because we had the benefit of having someone who loved us back at home after school. I remember how comforting it felt to be settled in with Grammy for a while before we got down to our homework. Grammy was perfectly happy just sitting at the kitchen table playing solitaire and listening to her favorite radio programs, all the while being on hand for us kids until Mom and Dad got home. I often feel a bit sorry for kids today who don't have that opportunity because their grandparents do not live close enough to interact as we did.

When we kids were in high school, Grammy began experiencing a number of health issues. She underwent a couple of major surgeries and never fully recovered from the second one. At one point, she was bedridden, at the mercy of all four of us, and had a health worker visit to meet her needs. After a while, it became necessary for her to be admitted to a local nursing home, an emotional experience for us all.

Because the nursing home was only minutes from our home, we had the opportunity to visit Grandma often, and were secure in the knowledge that all of Grammy's physical needs were being attended to. Over the year and a half that she was a resident at the nursing home, her condition worsened to the point where we knew that she did not have that much longer to be with us all. One night, we got a call from our family physician. Grammy was having difficulty breathing, and it looked like the end was near. My dad began the sad task of calling his three brothers to fill them in on what the doctor had told Dad. Not long after **he** got off the phone, the doctor called back with the unfortunate news of our grandmother's passing.

The following day, I had a very unique experience. As my mom had other details to take care of, it fell to me and my dad to make some purchases on Grammy's behalf, including the outfit she would be buried in. It was a truly surreal task. Since Grammy was not one to wear dresses, I chose a nice pair of pants and a beautiful blouse for her. I proceeded to the checkout area, and only when I had placed the blouse on the counter did I look at it closely enough to see … the Extra Button! The one the manufacturer sometimes attaches to clothing in case you lose the first one. The irony was not lost on me, as Grammy would not need one. Grammy, was that you trying to lighten my mood?

The Owl

Dad's brother Jimmy, his wife, Kally, and their daughter, Nastia, live near Charlotte, North Carolina. The weekend before Grammy passed, Jimmy flew up to visit her. Throughout her entire nursing home stay, Grammy never had much of a desire to be wheeled out into the sunshine on nice days, but this time, when Jimmy came to visit, she asked him to bring her outside for a few minutes of fresh air. Obviously, Jimmy and our whole family were so glad that he came up, because it turned out to be the final visit he would have with his mother.

On the night Grammy passed away, Jimmy and Kally had been asleep in their bedroom. They were suddenly awakened by the repeated sound of a hooting owl. Neither of them had ever heard an owl in the yard before, especially one so clear, and loud enough to awaken them. Very shortly after, the call came from my father, and they realized that Grammy had used a source of nature as a gentle way to say goodbye.

To be spiritual about owls, in some ancient stories they accompany a soul so it doesn't get lost on its journey to its reward.

Often since Grammy's passing, gifts that our family has exchanged with Jimmy and Kally have been with regard to owls. These pieces help us to keep Grammy's memory alive.

Grandma Comforts

I was on the five-year plan at college—in many situations it takes longer than the usual four years to get in all of your classes. At one point, I bought my father a mug that I spotted while out shopping one day— "College—the best seven years of my life!"

My parents had plans for a big party for me at the house, and naturally I was elated to be through with school and was looking forward to my first real job. It was exciting to think about celebrating with friends and family. As the big day got closer, Mom had only to finalize things with the caterer. Late on the night before, Dad called her into the living room. They both watched the Murphy's Law weather prediction: a foot of snow was predicted! This was an update from the much lighter amount previously announced. We figured that guests would be able to cope with a storm of two or three inches, but this was a different story.

Sure enough, during the night, the snow began to fall, and it got heavier by the hour. Not long after dawn, Mom placed a frantic call to the caterer. Unfortunately, he had already begun preparing all the food, so backing out was not an option. It was time to cross our fingers and say a prayer.

The caterer did end up making it through the snow in one piece. All that was left for us was to hope that, since no one called to cancel, that they could all get safely to our house. I spent the whole morning with the phone plastered to my ear, venting my worry to my friends. As it turned out, most of our invited guests were able to attend!

My mother made use of her pre-party nervous energy by vacuuming the house. As she was working in the living room, all of a sudden she was aware of a very brief but very powerful sweet scent all around her. *Wait a minute*, she thought to herself, *That's Grandma's favorite talcum powder!* She actually called out, "Grandma?" Prior to Grandma's death, she lived with us and, as she got less able to take care of her personal needs, my mother and I used to help her with her daily shower. That talcum powder scent was a very distinct one, and very personal to her alone.

It was a few days after the party that I shared something interesting with my mother. I had been a little hesitant beforehand to mention it. The previous week while I was at work teaching in my classroom, I was overcome by the same sweet scent my mom had described to me. As if that weren't enough, while driving home from work that day, I experienced that scent again—it filled my car for only a second or two, but just long enough to wrap me in the feeling that Grandma was keeping a watchful, loving eye on me at this exciting time in my life. She and I had always had a special bond—I was her first granddaughter and had been named in her honor.

The Head Scratcher

My parents were completely renovating a mid-century bathroom in their home, including the installation of a new floor.

My brother and sister-in-law had been temporarily living at the house, along with their two cats, a male and a female. The male, Buddy, was quite the explorer. One Saturday, the wooden sub-flooring was installed and, that night, Buddy went missing. He was just nowhere in sight. He didn't respond when they called him, even with the rattling of his cat treat bag. No Buddy. They left a bowl of food outside in case he had snuck out. No Buddy. They even took a ride around the neighborhood looking to see if he had been hit by a car, and was lying in the road. Still no Buddy. No sign of him all weekend.

Monday morning, my brother was getting ready for work in a bathroom below the one being renovated. He could have sworn he heard Buddy's meow. *Could it be?* Later on in the day, my sister-in-law thought she heard meowing coming from the bathroom being renovated. She went closer to the tiny opening in the floor through which a pipe was going to be fit and, sure enough, there was Buddy, down under the sub-flooring, scared as could be! She tried coaxing Buddy out for an hour and a half, finally deciding to light up her face with a flashlight so he could see that it was her. Knowing that he hadn't eaten in almost two days, my sister-in-law was able to toss down some food for him, and then she called the contractor to come over and take up the floorboards so Buddy could make his grand exit. Ah, the mystery of cats!

Maya was my Aunt Kally and Uncle Jimmy's dog.

Maya—A Lesson in Trust

My uncle and aunt in North Carolina wanted to adopt a dog, and they decided to check out a nearby shelter. There they saw many dogs of various sizes, but one in particular caught their eye. Maya was a female boxer, one that had visible signs of physical abuse on different parts of her body. They were told that this dog had an intense fear of men, stemming from the abuse she had apparently suffered at the hands of her previous owner. However, Aunt Kally and Uncle Jimmy felt a special connection with Maya as they stood there, wondering if this poor dog would end up having health issues in the future. That day, they left the shelter and thought over the situation that evening. During the night, the image of Maya's face came to them—her big, sad brown eyes flashed before them. When they woke up in the morning, they had experienced a change of heart, and decided to make a second trip to the shelter to give Maya a better, more secure home than she had come from.

After having been given a second chance at happiness, Maya proved to be an excellent watchdog, especially protective of my then-six year old niece, Nastia, Jimmy and Kally's daughter. It took Maya a while to warm up to any men who came into contact with her, but when she developed their trust, she had made a friend forever.

The Helping Hand

My mom's childhood home is one of several beautiful old houses on a street in a small New Jersey town. Across the street from Mom's is the home of a doctor and his wife, the Connors, who raised their large family at the same time Mom was growing up. Mrs. Connors ran a preschool out of their house, which Mom attended back in the day. One afternoon a few years ago, my mother was browsing social media to see if any of the Connors children were still in the area. She discovered that one of the daughters, Janet, lived close by, and Mom was able to make a lunch date with her, to reminisce a bit.

It turns out that Janet has a medical condition that makes getting around somewhat of a challenge, so Mom picked her up and they had a very nice lunch together. Afterward, Mom and Janet paid a visit to Mrs. Connors at the family homestead. Mom was very happy to be able to see and talk with her former pre-school teacher for a while, even bringing along a bouquet of flowers as a gift. At the time, Mrs. Connors was ninety-three years old, or should I say young! This is a woman who, as a teenager, had mastered the art of big-game hunting, which she learned from her father. The amazing thing, Mom said, was that Mrs. Connors was still quite lucid and, fortunately, self-sufficient. She lived by herself and spoke to Janet every day, just to check in.

When Janet and Mom arrived at the Connors home for what proved to be a very sweet visit, Mrs. Connors was at the side door, nearest to the driveway, ready to greet them. As per Janet's request, Mom had backed her car up as far as it could go, so that Janet could maneuver to her walker and carefully make it to the door. Just the sight of ninety-three-year-old Mrs. Connors holding the house door open for her daughter was a very profound moment for my mom. By rights, if parents even make it to that age, they are typically doted on by their children but, on that day, Mom was witness to the tenderness of the helping hand that Mrs. Connors extended to Janet. The love of a mother never dies, a message that was made very evident on that beautiful Wednesday morning in Mom's home town.

The Glass Half Full

Fast forward five years from my story of The Helping Hand. Mrs.
Connors was graced with the ability to remain in her own home to
live out the rest of her days. Shortly after her death at age ninety-eight,
her family held a memorial service, which my mom attended. It
was good for Mom to be able to reconnect with all of the Connors
siblings and express her sympathy for their loss. At the service, there
were the usual floral tributes and tables full of photographs that
documented special times in the family, but the one thing that stood
out to my mother was along the center wall of the room. There was
a beautiful framed photo of Mrs. Connors, and underneath that
was a table that held a glass tumbler half full of scotch. Apparently
she had enjoyed a glass each evening before dinner. To the left of
the photo and glass of scotch was something very unique, that my
mom had never seen at a memorial service. It was a large bottle of
Johnny Walker Red Label scotch, surrounded by tiny plastic cups.
It made for a fine opportunity to toast this wonderful woman from
my mom's home town. Mrs. Connors had made such a difference
and such a lasting impression on so many people whose lives she had
touched over the years. She was a loving mother to six children. She
had also been a public school teacher and a nursery school teacher
for more than fifty years. Education was her passion, and she served
her students well.

Coronavirus Delay

Building blocks in a zipped-up case. Idle child's table with two vacant chairs. A large plastic box full of his favorite books. An oval plastic train track with his treasured trains and their tenders placed lovingly inside. Four-year-old Nicholas is the one who taught his Gam Gam what a tender was even for … and now his toys wait for his return to my mom and dad's house, where Nick usually plays while my husband and I are at work.

Downstairs in the recreation room sits a large toy train that he hasn't been there to steer back and forth across the floor. My mother held onto strips of paper that served as tickets for each ride he gave her to whatever station she thought up.

Upstairs in Mom and Dad's family bathroom is a child's tooth-brush that has not been used for two months. And of course, hung by a plastic holder next to the toilet is Nick's potty seat, which also awaits his return.

My parents and my in-laws normally provide day care for our son but, since the middle of March 2020, two months ago, that has changed. Nick's father and I, who are teachers, have been home with him, and his things have stood idly by in both houses. Hopefully he will return to their care at some point over the next few months, because they miss him very much. We are just thankful that we are all healthy at this terrible time in history.

The Things You Learn...

The Fine Print Will Get You Every Time

Having been a credit-card user for years, I had reached the point where I had earned my first reward certificate. I chose a great restaurant and, when the coupon arrived, got all excited. Since I had a first date with a new guy coming that weekend, when he asked me where I might like to eat, I thought, *Cool! What could be better than to go there with him and end up with a discount coupon to offer him!* I was all set to impress. *What did I have to lose?*

The big night came and, on the drive to the restaurant, I mentioned that I had this discount coupon in my bag. It was for $50 off of a dinner. He was cool with it, and nicely surprised.

Once we got to our destination, we checked out the amazing menu: a steak for him and one of my favorite seafood dishes for me. I could feel us really clicking all through dinner—I love a guy with a great sense of humor. When we had finished eating, I slipped the dinner coupon out of my bag and passed it to my new guy. The waitress took the coupon and put the remainder on his credit card. We walked out hand in hand, satisfied from a fun evening with great food.

As he went to open his car door for me, we realized that someone was running toward us. It was our waitress, flagging us down. All out of breath, she was holding our dinner coupon in her hand, and explained that the discount only applied to their New York City restaurant. I waited in the car as my date returned to the front desk to take care of the balance. I should mention that he eventually became my husband, and we both look back on this night with a smile and a roll of the eyes.

Pinkerton, early 2000s.

The Second Chance

Several years ago, I was helping my mother trim the nails of our family cat, Pinky. Cats can become quite ornery where grooming is concerned, so Mom and I had found a way to accomplish this task without being maimed. We took Pinky out to the deck overlooking the back yard. I held him and tried to distract him by drawing his attention to any birds there might be, while Mom concentrated on carefully cutting just enough off his claws to be a decent trim.

One day a friend of mine came over to visit while Mom and I were trimming Pinky's claws out on the deck. This friend was in another room, and just as Mom was trying to place the nail cutter in a safe spot on Pinky's nail, my friend yelled out, "Aren't you afraid you will cut him?" And sure enough, for the first time in eight years, Mom succeeded in cutting too far on the nail and making Pinky bleed. And I mean bleed, to the point where we decided we needed the input of our veterinarian. Mom phoned her and was directed to place the cat's paw in flour. If, after she pulled it out, the paw was still bleeding badly, she should bring Pinky in for treatment. Fortunately, this did not happen and the bleeding was curtailed.

As a result of this incident, forever afterward, Pinky has not been agreeable to even being picked up by me, much less having any more pedicures. Animals never forget. That goes for good experiences and for bad. If it was a good experience they had with you, it's worth its weight in gold. They can see you twenty years later, and you'll be greeted warmly. A bad experience, however, after years and years, will still be remembered as such. Unlike humans, our maker did not bestow forgiveness on other species. I have always admired animals because, for example, they are not polluters like people (check any road exit ramp for plastic bags). They have a built-in respect for the environment. But, as we learned from our cat, you won't get a second chance if you cross them.

Maybe what we can learn from animals is caution when dealing with others.

The Praxis

In order to obtain a teaching license, I needed to pass an exam called the Praxis. It's a very involved exam with many parts, and is only given at certain places at certain times of the year. If you miss one, you have to wait a long while for another chance at it.

I had been a student teacher for a while, and my goal was to become a certified teacher with my own classroom of students, so I had to submit to be tested. I was supposed to get up early and go with a friend. We were to carpool.

Fate reared its ugly head, and I awoke on the morning of the Praxis feeling awful. I felt like I was coming down with something ugly and I knew I was in trouble, but I couldn't not show up. I would be disappointing family and boyfriend alike, plus I would have to wait months for another chance. I was dying! So much for chicken quesadillas for dinner last night— unfortunately my friends and I had chosen to eat food that didn't like me as much as I enjoyed it. My mother made me down a glass of juice, and then came the pep talk. She told me to just give it a shot—show up and make the effort.

I got to the school where it was being held and picked up my pencil. *Maybe this could work after all,* I thought. After about a minute, the words on the page started to move. I hadn't eaten breakfast and the walls in the classroom were starting to spin, but I forged ahead. Before I knew it, it was pencils down.

I managed to complete the exam, and fortunately I passed and did become a certified teacher. My mother, the cheerleader, had helped put me over the edge.

The Power of Smiley—The Original Emoji

In a previous story, I mentioned my mother's habit of using sticky notes to remind the family of something important. Somehow, this paranoid trait got passed along to me. Here is the tale of my first note.

I was speaking to my mother on the phone one day, and made an amazing revelation to her. My then-boyfriend (now my husband), Jon, had an issue with the bathroom plumbing at his condo, which he shared with a buddy of his. They were going to require the services of a plumber, because my boyfriend noticed that there was a problem with a bathroom faucet, and he had no clue as to how to get his roommate to always remember to treat it delicately. Jon was stressing over this dilemma when, without even thinking about it, I suggested that he leave a note near the bathroom sink. Then it hit me. Through no fault of my own, I was passing along my mother's advice ….

The most remarkable part of the conversation with Jon was when I suggested that, to relax his roommate about the situation, he should draw a smiley face on the note. That had been my mother's method of sweetening the pot, shall we say, when she wanted to make a point to us. Who could ever resist that little yellow face with the two perky eyes and cheesy grin? Jon's roommate fell for the bait, as did my brother and I for longer than I can remember. A goofy sticky note soon adorned the vanity in their condo. Persuasion in a smile.

The Purse-Size Tissue Pack

Shopping with my mom as a kid, as we walked down the paper-goods aisle, she always bought the little tiny plastic-wrapped mini-tissue packs. I teased her about it every time. "Mom, why don't you just buy the big boxes? Don't they last longer?"

She always answered, "I have my reasons. You'll see."

During the course of my normally messy childhood, there were countless times when I was out with her somewhere and she would reach into her purse, pull out a pack, and do her damage control to my face and hands. No rummaging around to, hopefully, find a loose tissue for this woman! And when we were planning a vacation or short trip somewhere, those little packs were always brought along.

One day while preparing for my honeymoon, I realized that I needed a trip to the store for the tiny-size versions of toiletries, and so on. Into the basket went the toothpaste, soap, shampoo, and deodorant. And then, as I got to the last basket in the row, I realized that I, too, was going to need what was inside. A very neatly-wrapped six pack of … tissues.

The Sticky Note

Ever since sticky notes were invented, my mother, like many other mothers in America, has relied on them. But in Mom's case, they were an obsession, exclusively the bright yellow ones. In my mind, I thought that a kitchen bulletin board of some kind would do the trick, but the beauty of sticky notes is that they can be placed all around the house, as needed. If Mom could have stuck them on the nosepiece of her eyeglasses she would have, but she never got quite that bad. I could just close my eyes and envision her at a twelve-step group meeting ... "Hi, I'm Marigene, and I love sticky notes ...."

Our sticky notes appeared on the fridge, in the bathroom, on her purse, and on our front door for the entire length of our formative years. It got so bad that, one day, while on a trip back home from Texas as an adult, my brother, the wise guy, created a series of notes much like the Burma Shave signs from along the highways back in the day. The progression began on our front door, saying "Just a note ... see second message in kitchen!"

Now comes the part where I experienced my turning point, that place where you find out that genetics can play their nasty hand before you realize what's happened to you. It was the first time, after moving into my own home, that I had something urgent to remind myself about. The message really was a crucial one, about something I needed to bring to work the next day.

What was I going to do? I couldn't set a timer, and I didn't want to shift responsibility and ask my husband to remind me (sometimes not so wise). Plus, it was back in the days before smart phones and Siri.

And so, I had no other choice—I was backed up against the wall of maternal what goes around comes around. So, I took a deep breath and proceeded to the kitchen gadget drawer–. There's one in every home. Okay, there was a pen … and something else—a three-by-three yellow paper sticky pad—staring brightly up at me in all its smugness. I tore off the top sheet and slammed the drawer closed in utter defeat. I had officially become part of the Sticky Note Club, thankfully one with no meetings to remember.

Grandfather Clock

To most people a generation before mine, the title of this chapter most likely brings to mind memories of childhood mornings spent enraptured by the TV show *Captain Kangaroo*. Grandfather Clock was a typical large standing clock that decorated the set of the show, except that he had large round eyes and a smile. Best of all, he spoke! In the course of the show, he would be asleep, but whenever a question arose for the children to learn something from him, the clock was approached by the Captain. He would say to the audience, "Let's ask Grandfather. Wake up, Grandfather!" And the eyes on the clock face would quickly open and close as if grandfather were momentarily startled. He would go into a poem and the questions would be answered with the gentle wisdom of an elderly relative. He was a sort of computer from back in the day, but with a wonderful, sweet edge.

My mother was browsing the Internet the other day and came upon a story. Apparently, when *Captain Kangaroo* was cancelled years ago, the props from the set were simply discarded. No one apparently gave a thought to any future interest that might be shown by the children of the 1950s and 1960s. An employee happened by the broadcast center loading dock where these beloved items had been tossed into a dumpster, and was startled to see the face of an old friend staring back at him. It was Grandfather Clock! Needless to say, Grandfather and several other pieces of the show's memorabilia were lovingly removed from their undeserved grave. The employee commented that it took a while to have the right people convinced that these items should be preserved in the archives of TV history. Some things are just sacred to each generation.

The Shoe on the Other Foot

In 2011, Hurricane Irene forced the river in my hometown to overflow its banks and, in addition to many others in the area, my childhood home was flooded. We were about a mile and a half from the river and through the years flood water had been confined to the basement, but Hurricane Irene was another story. The water actually reached the second floor of our split-level house, and necessitated some more-involved cleanup and reconstruction.

Our local church sprang into action, hosting dinners for the badly affected town residents, plus an amazing clothing, household cleaners, and children's toy donation pulled together quickly by a group of very considerate people.

My parents very thankfully attended one or two of the dinners during the exhausting initial cleanup days. They were among many other town residents in the same predicament, some a lot worse off than they were, damage wise.

Now, up to this point in time, our family had been fortunate enough to never suffer any major catastrophes, and neither had we ever been on the receiving end of area charity. So, at the first church dinner, Mom and Dad felt very awkward as they ate and shopped through the donated items—the shoe was on the other foot, as they say.

The auditorium held a number of donation bins, and Mom knew that cleaners would be a big help back at the house. Among the items in that bin was a partially used bottle of disinfectant liquid cleaner. Because the bottle was not a new, full one, some might feel that the donor was getting rid of something they tried and did not like very much. However, to my mom, the receiver, it was something she was quite grateful for. Someone's castoff had brightened another person's day.

Move Along

My parents once went on a chartered bus to Atlantic City with some people from work. While there, my father was sitting at a slot machine and a very disheveled-looking man approached him, asking him for any money he could spare. The man was wearing a hooded sweatshirt with the hood up, which covered his overgrown hair. On his feet were an old, broken pair of shoes, held together by layers and layers of duct tape. As my startled father began to say, "I'm sorry," he and the stranger were approached by a security agent from the casino, who asked this homeless man to "Move along, please." My mom mentioned that she had also seen this man later on in the day, making his way along the casino floor and heading to the men's room. Mom said that the incident made her appreciate the nice, hot shower she had taken that morning—routine as any other day and complete with fresh-smelling cleansers that this man had apparently not enjoyed for quite some time. Such a dichotomy is Atlantic City—full of those who are blessed and those who crave. I had the same reaction to beggars lying along Fifth Avenue in New York when my family used to take the train in on the day after Thanksgiving. The highs and lows of life on one long sidewalk.

The Museum Visit

Recently, my parents took a road trip to Washington, D.C. One of the places they visited was the Air and Space Museum, which houses, among other things, many historic aircraft. It's a huge three-story hangar where you can view the vehicles from all different angles and levels. While they were walking along, they came to the area with various aircraft (e.g., bombers, helicopters) used in Vietnam during the 1960's conflict. One of the pieces was what is commonly referred to as a Huey, a medical helicopter that airlifted our wounded military out of the field of combat.

As my mother was reading the explanations posted for tourists, she noticed a man and a teenage boy standing nearby. The older man was reminiscing with the boy (his grandson, perhaps?) about how he had flown many rescue missions in a Huey just like that one during his tour of duty.

Mom felt moved to tell him, "Thank you for your service!" What made the incident even more meaningful was that my parents' visit took place over Veterans Day weekend.

The Power of Touch

My parents were at church for mass recently, when the priest used this sermon. My mother found it very inspirational.

A wealthy woman once approached the lady who most people know was famous for working with the poor in India. The wealthy woman had been observing the extreme poverty that people were living in and wanted to make a contribution to the cause. She offered to write a blank check for whatever might be needed, but was politely offered an alternative. She was instead taken by the hand and brought to a very small child. This little girl was among the many who were very ill or dying from lack of food, water, and personal attention. The woman was asked to take care of this little girl and her physical needs. The girl needed feeding and hands-on care—a bath and a lot of one-on-one attention.

The priest used the term "skin hunger" to describe the poor child's condition. We all need the power of touch in our lives.

My parents provide much of the daycare for my son, Nicholas. When my husband and I leave him in their care each morning, Nick knows that we will be returning later in the day and that he is good hands with people who love him. This was not always the case. Several months ago, there were instances where my son was devastated to see us leave and have the door close behind us. Nicholas sobbed his little heart out until either my mom or dad picked him up onto their lap and consoled him in their arms, trying their best to distract him from his sadness. Time and loving arms have served to soothe him.

There are people who volunteer to cuddle babies at hospitals in order to boost the babies' health. These babies were either born prematurely or have serious health issues. The touch that the volunteers provide is an invaluable help. Maybe it's not even to hold the child, but even just to reach a finger inside an incubator or stroke a tiny belly when hospital staff is not always available. As often as possible, it's the solution to that skin hunger.

Just Fill the Thing Out Already!

In 2010 there was a national census taken, where the U.S. government mailed a form to every household in America. It contained ten easy-to-answer questions, and you were to return the form as soon as possible. I have always been the kind of girl who does not have a lot of tolerance for—or maybe is intimidated by—official-looking paperwork. So what did I do? I, like other people who come home from work and rush hurriedly through their mail, simply tossed the form along with the day's postal junk. *That took care of that,* I thought. Wrong!

I have the kind of parents who had a conservative, do-it-by-the-book upbringing, so they were both very concerned when I mentioned my deed some time later. Dad advised me to find out who to call to receive another form, and I did so, not relishing the thought of being fined. Only, the form never arrived. So, what did do? I went on about my business for a few weeks, hoping that governmental red tape would take a while to sort it out.

At the time, I lived in a high-security condo complex, where no one can surprise you by being at your door when you come home. I was always alerted that a visitor needed to come up on the elevator. One night I had gotten in from seeing a movie with a friend. It was about 8:30, and I was settling down for the evening when I heard a knock on my door. I didn't have any particular friends in the complex, as most residents just came and went during the day, so it was a little scary to know that someone was out in my hallway needing me. When the management office had messages for residents, they left a printed computer sheet in everyone's door. That made this incident quite an adrenaline rush!

On opening the door, I saw a man I did not recognize, on bended knee writing something on paper. He explained that he was from the Census Bureau and was here about my form. After a few seconds, my normal heart rate resumed. He got the information he came for, and I got the message to take a second look at future mailings!

The Silver (with by-products) Ring, or My Carrie Moment

I had been dating my new boyfriend for almost a year and a half. Things were getting serious and, around that time, I had admired a certain message ring that a well-known jewelry company sells. The ring has "I love you" written on it several times around the band, and the ad said that it was made of sterling silver. To my delight and surprise, not long afterward my boyfriend surprised me with the ring!

That weekend, my parents had a party and my boyfriend and I were there. As I was sitting with my parents and their friends, I wanted to show them my new ring. I realized then that my ring finger had been itching for most of the day. As I looked down at the finger with the ring on it, I noticed that there was a black stain at the base of my finger under the ring. This meant that I was allergic to this jewelry!

I called the company, letting them know my disappointment and displeasure. Apparently, the ring is not 100 percent silver, but is also composed of nickel, which is known to cause skin irritation in jewelry. I was not amused. At the time, there was no other ring design, either on the Internet or in stores, quite like this particular one. That was the beauty of coming across this ring and actually having it bought for me by someone so important in my life.

Since that day, I have made several phone calls to the company, in an attempt to figure out a way that I could still be able to wear this cherished ring. They do not do custom orders for less than a five-figure amount, so that was out of the question. Needless to say, it was not a productive phone experience.

Finally, a supervisor suggested that I wear the ring Carrie style. It was time to educate this supervisor. Being a die-hard fan of the show featuring the character Carrie, I knew the reason why she did not wear the ring on her finger. She had gotten an engagement ring from her boyfriend, but was not ready to accept his proposal. So she wore his ring on a chain around her neck. That way it could be close to her heart, but not yet a commitment. This was not going to fly in my case. I had no problem clueing in the world on my own relationship status.

As beautiful as the ring was, I had to return it to the store...

The Shattered Glass

At one point in my life, I moved into an apartment—the first time I had ever lived away from home. I had even lived at home while attending college. So began the adventure of independence. The door was wide open for things you remember that your mother once said.

One night I was opening the freezer to get some ice for my glass of water, when I hit the glass on the fridge somehow. The next thing I knew, there was blood and glass all over the place. I should also tell you that I don't always do things slowly or carefully, this being one of the times when I should have.

Living at home, my first instinct would have been to yell for my mother to help me with the first aid. Then the light bulb went on. *Sweetheart, you're on your own for this one!* So I got my own stinkin' Band Aid, and remembered that the best way to clean up small shards of glass was to get out a slice of bread to press down on them with. That little maternal voice in my head had kicked in ….

Who's Raising These People?

When we were kids, Mom and Dad brought us to the Museum of Natural History, where one of the exhibits was The Evolution of Man. You know the one I mean. It starts out with the ape man, and moves on up to homo sapiens, the present-day dude.

I'm sure that, even in the world of the cave man, parents of children had to set some kinds of behavioral standards for interacting with their neighbors. One would naturally assume that, by the twenty-first century, people had gotten the hang of the do-unto-others-as-you-would-have-them-do-unto-you concept. It doesn't appear so. Once in a while, you come across someone who never got the message.

Take the other day. I was on my way into a local coffee shop. It has an outside swinging-door entrance and an inside one. There was a gentleman ahead of me on my way in. He very matter-of-factly opened the outer door and just let it shut behind him. Then he let me know in no uncertain terms that chivalry was dead, flat lined with no pulse. The inside door also swung closed in my face, and I knew then that this guy was probably doomed to be single for the remainder of his days. I snuck a peak. *That's what I thought, no wedding ring. He will most likely never get a smile of thanks for a chair pulled out while dining with a date.* That was my consolation thought as I purchased my cup of coffee that day.

While I'm on the subject of manners, where did the ball drop on finding a trash can for one's wrappers when one is out in public? Mom would always make us carry them in our pockets until we found one. End of rant.

Rug Pads

When I was a kid, my mother bought a giant piece of flat foam that she said was for underneath the new rug in our front entrance hallway. I had never seen a piece that big so, later on in the day, I watched as mom laid it out on the floor. She placed the hallway rug on top of the foam so she could measure how big a piece she would need. The necessity for this safety measure never hit home until the week after I got my own apartment. Had it all decorated just the way I liked it, with a beautiful big rug at the entrance. It looked amazing on my shiny new rented hardwood floors!

Later the same day, I went out to food shop, as I was going to host a big breakfast in the morning for some friends. I came up with the idea for Omelette Day, and feedback on my plan was looking good. I figured out what I would need from the store and set about my task.

On my way out of the supermarket dairy section, wheeling my cart in place at the check-out counter, my attention was drawn to a display of gorgeous bouquets of fresh flowers already set into cute little glass vases full of water. *These would be great*, I thought, *for the middle of the breakfast table*. So I had four of them put into an open box and made my way to my car. Singing along with the radio on the way home, I was glad to hear the weatherman talking about how great it was supposed to be tomorrow, the Day of the Omelets. *Yay!*

Swinging around the corner to my street, I pulled into my apartment driveway and grabbed my purse. I got out and picked up the two bags and the big box of flower vases. Maybe by now you can sense where this is going. With my purse over my shoulder and my arms overloaded, I unlocked my apartment door and called out a greeting to my cat. That was right before the accident. My shoe caught the slippery rug at just the right angle for it to slide far enough so that I landed with a thud on my butt. To add insult to injury, anyone with a cat for a pet knows that they cannot stand to be wet, much less covered with the gooey mess of broken eggs. It was not a pretty sight.

In trying to right myself, I realized that I could not move my right leg. Great, my ankle was swelling up like a balloon.

"911. What is your emergency?"

The Paint Brush

I had been married for several months when my husband and I decided it was time to update his condo that I had moved into. The place, up to this point his bachelor pad, needed some freshening up, which was well underway. A fresh coat of paint was necessary, and so we got to work.

Thankfully, my parents had agreed to give us a hand, and we had a productive day, starting on the living room first. It's always more pleasant when you have help with projects like that. Many hands do make light work, as the saying goes. As we went along, we realized how much just a simple coat of paint can really transform a room.

When the job was completed, the paint can was covered, and four tired people were ready to sit down to takeout pizza. My mother said, "Oh, do you have a piece of aluminum foil?"

"Sure, Mom," said I. "What for?"

So mom told me how I could wrap the brush full of paint in foil until the next day, in case the walls needed touching up. It would keep the paint from drying out. She added that you can't always tell where these areas that needed to be touched-up might be until the paint dries and you see things in a different light.

I said, "Mom, really? After two coats of paint I'm done with this. Just toss the brush, please!"

The next day, my husband and I looked over the job and then just looked at each other. Five or six different spots that we missed appeared on our dry walls, just for spite, I was sure. In the kitchen garbage can sat a dried up paintbrush full of Latte Beige, which would now have to be soaked and cleaned before we could get to the touch ups.

The Hood

Like most young children, when it's cold out or there's a slight drizzle outside, my mother would be vigilant enough to yell out, "Hey, you kids better grab something with a hood!" She never missed a storm prediction.

One day my husband and I were planning to go into the city to see the sights, and we were bringing my mom along. Of course, we checked our phones for up-to-date weather reports. I noticed the possibility of a rain shower, so what did I do in spite of myself? I texted Mom that she would be wise to carry a jacket with a hood. Then, after about five seconds, I followed up with another text: "That was mother-daughter reversal at its finest, wasn't it Mom?"

The Summer Sweater

For as long as I can remember, and most likely for years before I was even around, my mother has taken a sweater along with her wherever she goes. A just-in-case item.

Could be ninety-five degrees outside, but a sweater is either planned ahead of time or a last-minute grab for her. The reasoning is, "You never know if it's air conditioned inside or if the weather turns at night!"

Right, Mom. Go ahead, off to wherever, looking like somebody I don't want to be seen with because of what you're carrying. My father had just gotten used to it over the years. He doesn't even comment anymore, to keep the peace.

So now it's the summer, and my husband and I are invited to a party at his parents' house. They have a pool, and it was a very hot day. I wore my bathing suit with shorts, threw on some flip flops, and we were all set to go. It was then that I felt a surge of genetics kick in, as I found myself making a dash for my closet to grab ... a sweater? Absolutely, because their house is air-conditioned, and you never know if the weather gets cooler at night ....

Quick–How Many Items in a Dozen? No Cheating!

One day when my parents and I were visiting my brother, we decided to order pizza and wings for dinner. My brother called a local pizzeria to place the order. He told the pizza guy that he needed thirty-six wings. The guy responded that wings only come in packs of twenty-four or forty-eight. He was really confused about what to do. So my brother said, "Couldn't you just split up a set of twenty-four and take twelve out in order to give us the three dozen?"

The guy responded, "Whoa—I'm not that good at math!" My brother asked to speak with the manager, and that's what was needed to get our extra dozen wings. It's a scary world.

The Gift-Wrap Menagerie

I was at Mom's house one day while she was sorting things out in the basement. In one area was a large assortment of items used for gift-wrapping purposes. A big box of different kinds of papers and bows, and two or three containers of all-occasion bags with different colored tissue paper. I said, "Mom, this whole area is just gift wrap storage? Look how much room it takes up! No wonder there is so little space in the basement!"

She replied, "You know, it's just one of those things. You never know when you might need a gift done up. Saves a lot of time."

About six months later, a last-minute invitation came for my husband and me. We were asked to attend a party that night at a good friend's home. I rushed out to buy a really nice gift. Time was kind of tight, and I was thinking that with everything else I needed to do that day, I would never make it home in time to wrap it nicely. I found myself on my phone in the store, calling … Mom. "I hope you are home. I have a little problem. Can I swing by? I had to buy a quick gift for a party tonight, and maybe you have some nice paper and a bow? It shouldn't take long."

Fast forward to last month. The old water heater in our condo sprang a leak, and we had to make an emergency appointment with a plumber. In preparation for the installation of the new appliance, it was necessary to empty out its storage closet. After the plumbers were through with the job, my husband

and I proceeded to replace the mammoth amount of stuff that had been in that tiny enclosure. It seemed an impossible task, as things accumulate over time. Among the many items was a gift bag full of other gift bags and wrapping paper.

"Well, this thing can go!" my husband said to me.

I replied, "Are you kidding? Do you have any idea how much these bags and paper would cost to replace? You never know when you'll need a bag, you know!"

The Button Box

In 2020 when the Coronavirus struck, there was massive need for face masks all over the world. At the time that the virus hit, there was no cure for what became known as a pandemic, which was spread extremely easily through saliva droplets and by touching one's hands to one's face.

In the town where my mother lived was a woman named Kim who took it upon herself to construct masks from her house to help fill this drastic need. She started out with a few orders and, before long, she was receiving international emails for her help. She even got a request from a group of monks in Hawaii, her most impressive request to that point.

Mom had been following this woman's page on Facebook. She and many others had been dropping off materials that could be cut up and used to make the masks.

Kim worked many hours a day and into the night to fulfill the growing number of orders she received. One day my mom noticed that Kim had put out a call on Facebook for anyone who might have extras of a certain size button in their homes. For individuals like doctors or nurses who wear them hour after hour, face masks proved uncomfortable to wear with loops that attached behind the ears. So, it worked better if the connection was behind the head. The ear loops attached to a piece of material that buttoned behind the head. That way the pressure could be taken off the ears and the mask fit more comfortably.

Once she saw the Facebook post, my mom immediately remembered that my grandma Vickie (Grammy) used to save extra buttons in a special wooden box. Mom had an immediate inspiration. She went upstairs to retrieve the box and, in sorting through the group of buttons, she was able to come up with thirty-four of them to donate. Mom told me that she could just imagine that, if Grammy were alive, she would quickly be on her way upstairs to her room to locate that button box. It would have been an honor on Grammy's part to have done so, as it was for my mom to contact Kim and donate almost three dozen of the badly needed buttons.

The Desire for Privacy

As my pregnancy with my son rolled into its ninth month, I often discussed with my husband that I couldn't wait till we were finally a family of three, on our own, just relaxing and enjoying each other. How exciting it would be for us new parents in this new adventure! After all, when babies are new, it seemed they pretty much just eat and sleep, with a few diaper changes in between. I would daydream about the adorable little boy we were anticipating, and how he would probably take his evening bottle and then drift off until morning.

I talked to my husband about how important privacy seemed, and we passed along this wish to our respective parents. Just the two of us bonding with the baby for a few weeks would be the perfect way to start out our time as a new family.

Except that our son hardly slept for those first weeks. He was not comfortable nursing, so he became a formula baby, but what did we know? We were afraid to give him too many ounces at a time, so when we put him down to sleep, he woke right back up before too long. Sleep deprivation is a killer. Not so much a situation of postpartum depression, just lack of a proper amount of sleep. There I was, trying to take care of the baby during the night to let my husband sleep so he could be rested for work, but I was obviously also up during the day with the baby. It was messing with my head something awful.

"Mom, can you give me a hand with the baby? I really need a rest!" Privacy doesn't always work after your firstborn appears! And some of Mom's infant-care pointers didn't hurt, either.

The Free Swing

I gave birth to a little boy in 2016 (a FOMO child, as it turns out, one with Fear of Missing Out). He took very short daily naps, if at all, and he was the type that required almost a jostling motion when he was cranky and needed to be held. I kidded my mother that this was probably a result of our condo at the time being a third-floor walkup, requiring me to climb up lots of stairs each day. Apparently, throughout my pregnancy, my baby was used to a lot of up and down motion.

When it was time to visit the baby supply store, where they give you a clicker and you choose the items you would like to have on your baby registry, my husband and I decided on a baby chair with a nice, gentle, side-to-side motion. It looked like a good one and was a little bit on the expensive side, so we selected it, thinking that a higher price would guarantee the best chair in the store.

It was great to receive the chair at my baby shower, and I happily set it up in the living room of our condo. I have previously mentioned the fact that we discovered how much motion our son needed to relax him and send him off to sleep. Unfortunately, even on high power, the chair in question was not going to cut it. Way too gentle for this boy. It took three more tries and a couple more store returns to find a chair that would work for us.

In the meantime, my mother received a phone call from the mother of a coworker. The coworker's children had outgrown the infant stage of baby equipment, and her mom was asking if I would like to have some items she had available, including a baby chair. So Mom was smart enough to say, "Sure, they would be very much appreciated! Thanks so much for thinking of us!" That afternoon, the woman dropped off the items she had mentioned. I came to visit my mother the next day with the baby and, of course, had to try him out in the baby chair. It was amazing. He immediately took to this two-speed swinging chair that was a quarter of the cost of the original one! Some things you can't predict.

The Tuck-In

In almost two and a half years, my husband and I had never left our son overnight with a sitter for any reason. It just seemed to be an imposition on family members to ask them to give that much time to us. However, a very good friend of mine got engaged and asked me to be in her wedding, which I was very excited about! That was when I knew that, for practical purposes, it was time to tweak our son's nighttime routine. At a certain time, he was used to a few minutes of playtime in the bath, then getting into his pajamas, and finally settling down in his bedroom with a book that I would read to him. Some nights, he, naturally, was fussy, and he developed a ploy that got me back into his bedroom for a minute. He was still used to having a pacifier when he went in for the night, so he would fling the pacifier out of the crib onto the rug, and then call me to come in and help him get it back. Therefore, he was stalling sleep and having another moment with Mommy.

I approached my parents about the idea of possibly staying overnight at our condo with Nick, and they were fine with it. So my husband and I had my parents come over for dinner and stay for the bath routine for Nick. My mother actually did bath time, following my general routine, and then dried him in a towel and took him into his bedroom. There she got him into his pajamas, offered him a pacifier, and sat him down on her lap in his rocking chair for a last book reading of the day.

My mom said it was such a special few minutes for her. As the saying goes, she was in her glory just sharing this routine with our little guy. Nick went right into bed after my mom said "I love you" to him, answering with "Love you too!"

I was actually a little jealous that Mom had aced the nighttime tuck in! Nick spent about half an hour in the crib just settling himself down for the night. The task had gone off without a hitch for Grandma. We repeated this routine with my mom at the helm another couple of times before the actual wedding weekend, which really put my mind at ease. We were very happy to realize that the world was not going to end if my husband and I were otherwise occupied for one night!

The Butterfly

Several years ago, soon after the passing of my grandfather, my mom received a gift from Sandy, her office manager at the time. It was a stained glass sun catcher in the form of a butterfly, with a message hanging below—Time Heals. Naturally, our family had been very sad and upset following Grandpa's passing, and Sandy's gift was such a comfort to my mother. She brought the piece home from work and hung it on the sliding glass door leading out to the deck. It allowed us all to enjoy seeing the sunlight shining through the beautiful piece, and it reminded Mom of her good friend each day.

A visit from a friend.

Sandy was the kind of person who would give you the shirt off her back, and help anyone who was down or in need of some friendship or kindness. A few years later, Sandy was diagnosed with cancer. She grew more tired by the day at work, and after a few months she was not physically able to continue on the job. One day Sandy left for a doctor's appointment and was never able to return to the office.

Sandy continued to communicate with my mother and her other coworkers for a time, until her illness got the better of her. One day my mother got the dreaded text from a woman at the office to call this woman back. Mom knew right away that Sandy must have passed. Working in such a small office, all the women had become very good friends, and Sandy was, and still is, greatly missed.

A few months after Sandy's death, my mother was out on the deck and the strangest thing happened. She looked up at the house wall and there, perched on a brick, was a beautiful black and blue butterfly. Mom was able to get unusually close to just appreciate this butterfly for a few minutes, without it even flinching. It even remained on the house wall long enough for mom to grab her phone from the house and take a quick photo! Immediately she felt a strong connection to Sandy, and this moment felt like a little message from her friend.

In the course of its life, a butterfly goes through stages. The growing pains of a caterpillar, and then its liberation as a free spirit. In various social media posts, Sandy's widowed husband has said, "fly free … " as a loving message to her. Mom's butterfly visit has given her the confidence that her good friend is, indeed, enjoying a new freedom.

Exiting a Movie Theater

My mother always used to have an interesting opinion about going to the movies. She realized that, when you go into a theater with all the normal daily cares and concerns you carry with you, the experience temporarily transforms you. You sit, absorbed in the movie for a couple of hours and, when you leave and step back out onto the street, you return to your normally scheduled life. I never really stopped to think about what she meant by that, but now I do.

Stepping back into reality gives you a chance to change the things that need changing, and to just be thankful for those that are good.

Here is a photo of my parents from a while back.

My Mom and Dad, 1990s.